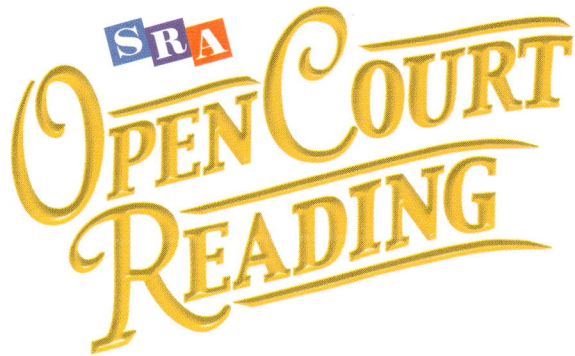

Dogs and Cats

A Division of The McGraw·Hill Companies

Columbus, Ohio

www.sra4kids.com

SRA/McGraw-Hill
A Division of The **McGraw·Hill** Companies

Copyright © 2002 by SRA/McGraw-Hill.

All rights reserved. Except as permitted under the United States Copyright Act, no part of this publication may be reproduced or distributed in any form or by any means, or stored in a database or retrieval system, without prior written permission from the publisher.

Printed in the United States of America.

Send all inquiries to:
SRA/McGraw-Hill
8787 Orion Place
Columbus, OH 43240-4027

ISBN 0-07-569462-X

3 4 5 6 7 8 9 DBH 05 04 03 02

Sam has dogs.
His dogs are Bigs and Figs.

Sam has cats.
His cats are Bugs and Mugs.

Bigs does not like Bugs.
Bugs does not like Bigs.

Mugs does not like Figs.
Figs does not like Mugs.

Sam hugs Figs, Mugs, Bugs, and Bigs.

Figs, Mugs, Bugs, and Bigs all like Sam.